Gordon Jacob

FIVE PIECES

for solo clarinet

Oxford University Press

To Georgina Dobrée

FIVE PIECES FOR CLARINET

(unaccompanied)

GORDON JACOB

1. Preamble

© 1973 Oxford University Press

Printed in Great Britain
OXFORD UNIVERSITY PRESS, MUSIC DEPARTMENT, GREAT CLARENDON STREET, OXFORD OX2 6DP

Photocopying this copyright material is ILLEGAL.

2. Waltz

3. Homage To J.S.B.

4. Soliloquy

5. Scherzo and Trio

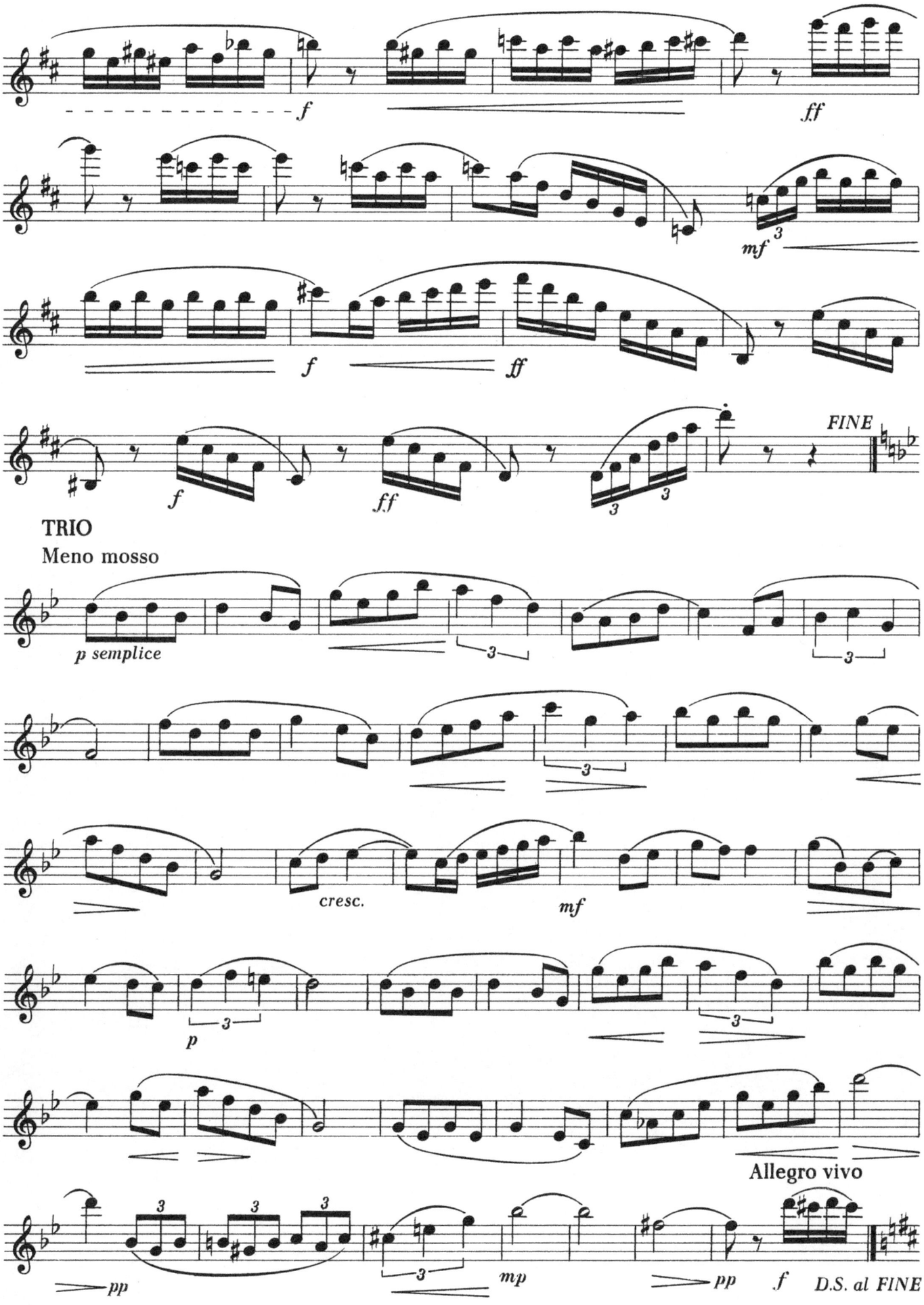

Reproduced and printed by
Halstan & Co. Ltd., Amersham, Bucks., England

Engraved by PWM

ISBN 978-0-19-357368-0